BLACK WOMEN AMPLIFIED

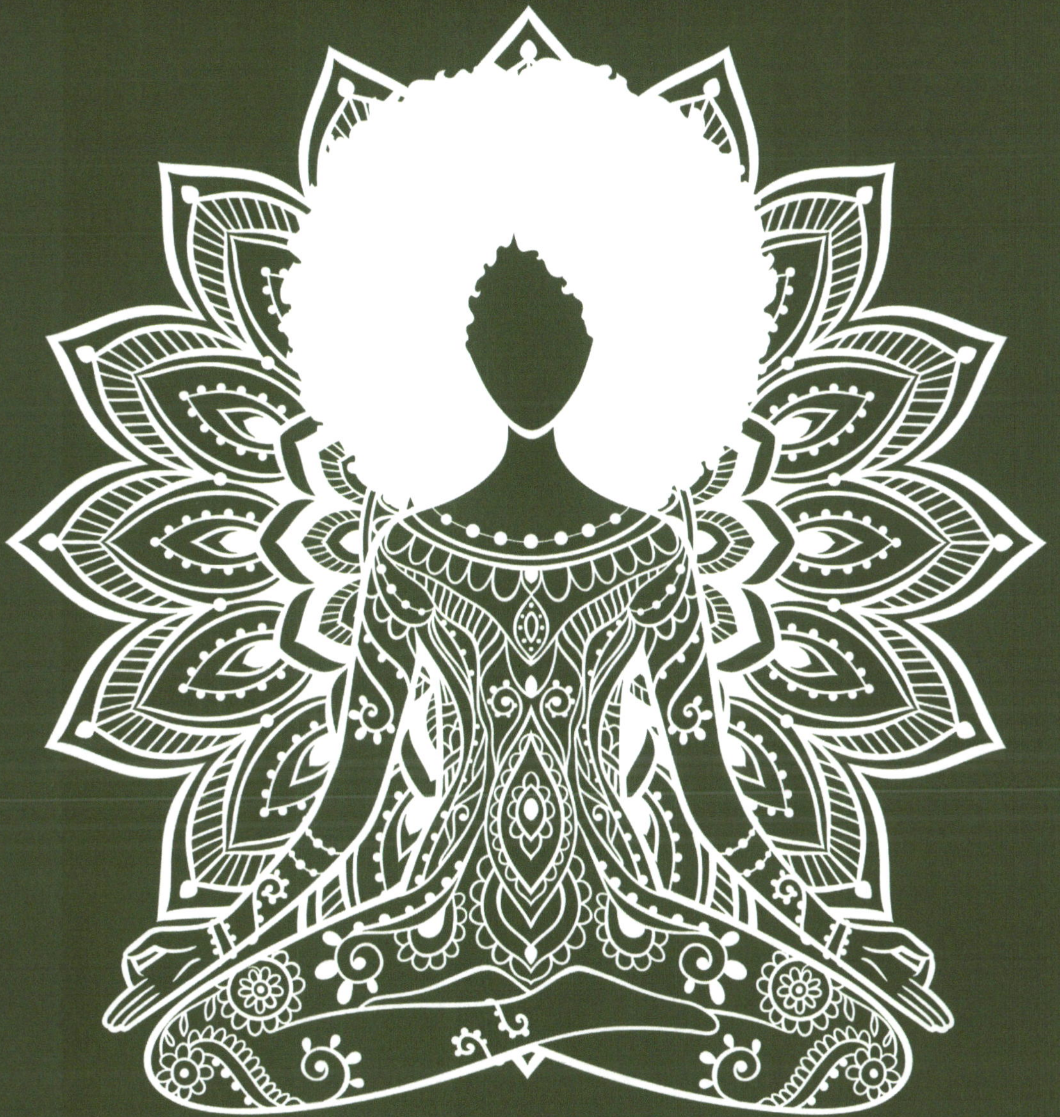

SELF LOVE

A SELF-DISCOVERY JOURNAL

& COLORING BOOK©

by Monica Wisdom HQ

WWW.BLACKWOMENAMPLIFIED.COM

ABOUT US

Monica Wisdom, the founder of Black Women Amplified and Monica Wisdom Coaching, aims to help people recognize their innate ability to create a life filled with love and self-worth. Her ultimate goal is for individuals to experience profound self-love. More information about Monica Wisdom and her companies can be found at www.monicawisdomhq.com.

Self-care is something that we often overlook, but it is crucial for our overall well-being. Taking time to focus on ourselves can help us clear our minds, reduce stress, and improve our mental health.

By setting aside time to answer the guided questions, you can gain insight into your emotional and mental state. Having a journal and pen ready to document your experiences will also help you keep track of your progress.

Remember to be comfortable and have snacks ready if needed, as this will help you relax and focus. If you can, try to set aside 20 minutes every morning to focus on yourself. You can add meditation and journaling to expand the experience and make it even more beneficial. Most importantly, have fun with it! Remember that you are worth taking this time for yourself.

Love and Light,

Monica Wisdom

I AM GRATEFUL

I AM WORTHY.

I AM INNOVATIVE.

I AM POWERFUL.

I AM BOLD.

I AM EVOLVING.

I AM BECOMING.

I AM ABUNDANT.

I AM DIVINE.

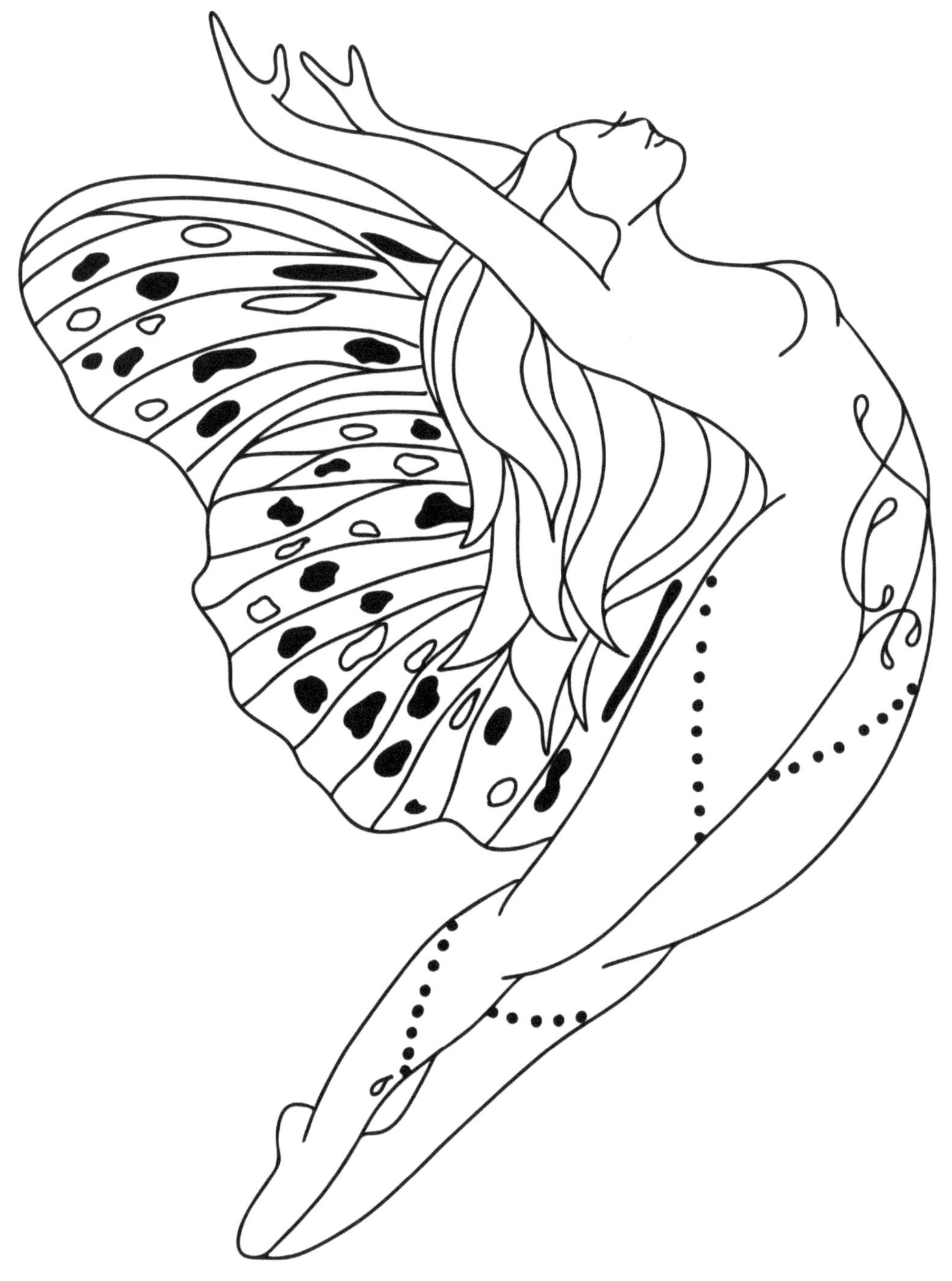

I AM FREE.

I AM WHOLE.

I AM COURAGEOUS.

I AM COMPLETE.

I AM WORTHY.

I AM BALANCED.

I AM A MIRACLE.

I AM BRAVE.

I AM ME.

Self Discovery
PART ONE

How to use this template?

The first step to finding out about your deeper motives, obstacles and desires is to write down simple statements about yourself. Finish the sentences below as accurately as you can - take your time and be honest!

01 I feel most comfortable when...

02 I feel most stressed when...

03 I can be my authentic self when...

04 One of my best memories is...

05 One of my toughest memories is...

06 The most useful things I've learned so far are...

Self Discovery
PART TWO

01 I wish I could...

02 I wish I had...

03 I wish I'd be more...

04 I wish I knew...

05 I wish I would regularly...

06 I think my biggest obstacles are...

07 I think life should be about...

08 I think the first step I should take to get to that life is...

Self-Realization

01   What steps have I taken to get to know true self?

02   What steps do you need to take to commit to knowing yourself?

03   Asking the Tough Question: What Scares You the Most?

Self-Love

01 What do you love most about yourself? Name at least ten.

02 Is naming ten things you love about something difficult? Why or why not?

03 Could you express these ten attributes to someone else? To whom and why?

Love, Light and Inspiration

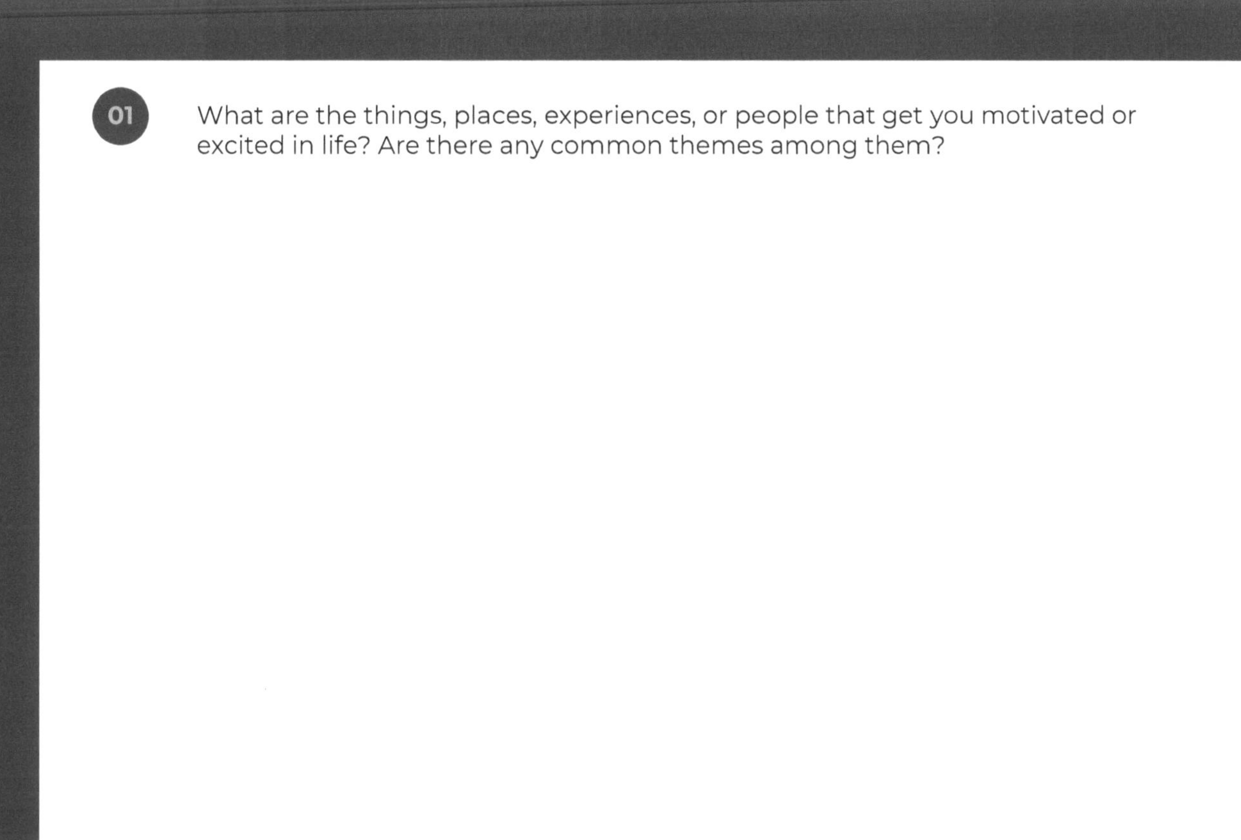

01 What are the things, places, experiences, or people that get you motivated or excited in life? Are there any common themes among them?

02 What steps can you take and changes can you make to manifest more of these things, experiences, and people in your life?

Who am I?

Directions

We all have an idea of who we are. Many of us are not clear on how to describe our strengths and character. Think about the qualities you love best about yourself and what is the core of who you are. There is no right or wrong. This is simply about getting to know yourself better.

adventurous	enthusiastic	imaginative	practical
affectionate	energetic	jovial	respectful
ambitious	exciting	kind	responsible
athletic	educated	knowledgeable	reliable
attentive	emphatetic	loyal	serious
analytical	easy going	loving	spiritual
brave	faithful	lucky	spontaneous
benelovent	friendly	mysterious	sensitive
charming	funny	mature	self-reliant
compassionate	focused	modest	sociable
calm	flexible	motivated	sweet
capable	forgiving	optimistic	straightforward
caring	grateful	obedient	strategic
charismatic	generous	orderly	talented
clever	gentle	open-minded	tactful
competetive	helpful	organized	tasteful
confident	hopeful	outgoing	thanful
courageous	happy	polite	tolerant
curious	humorous	patient	trusting
determined	independent	precise	thoughful
disciplined	inspiring	popular	useful
dependable	intelligent	proud	wise
daring	integrity	persistant	witty

 **01** Write down your top ten strengths

02 What are your biggest weaknesses?

Know Thyself

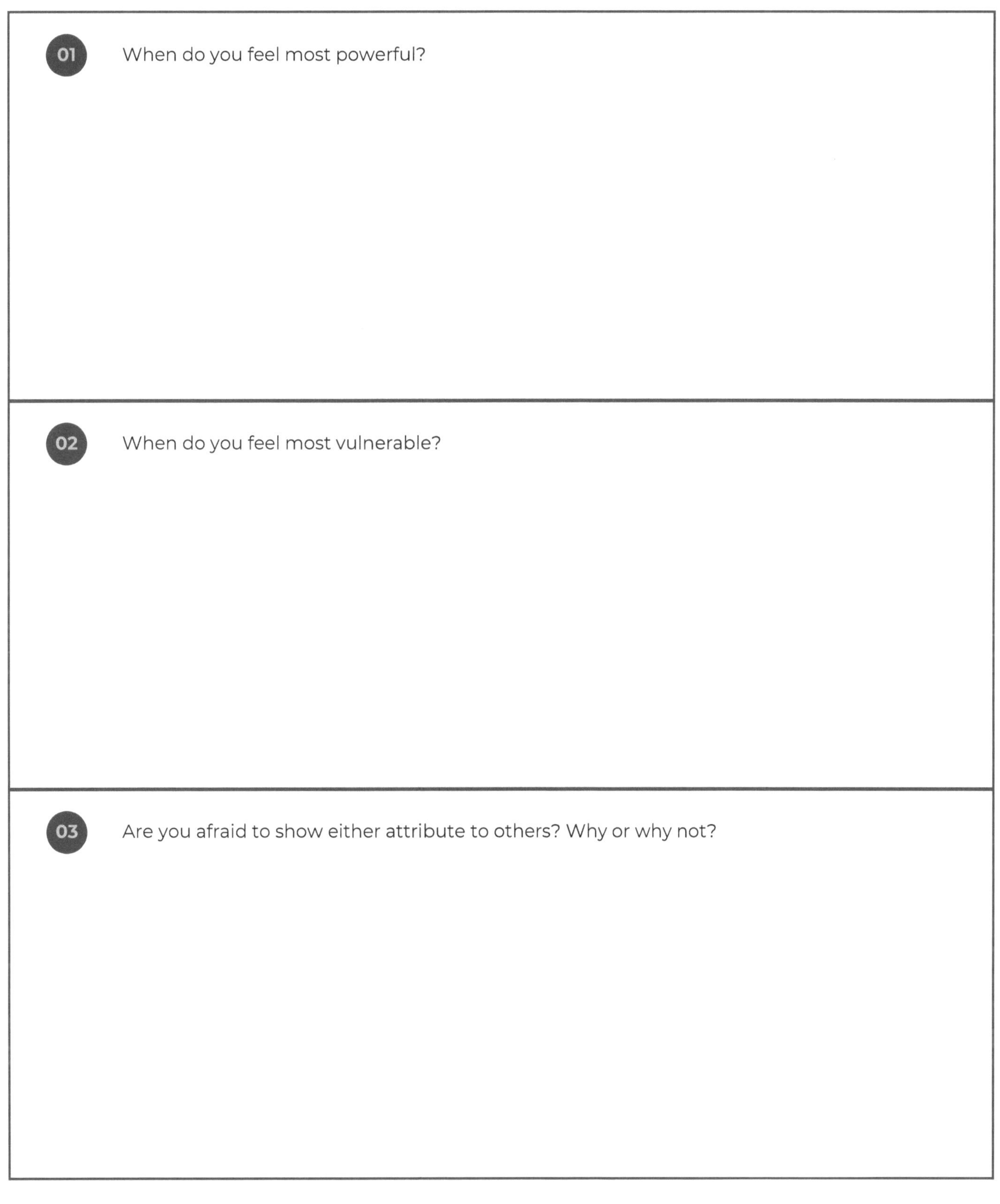

01   When do you feel most powerful?

02   When do you feel most vulnerable?

03   Are you afraid to show either attribute to others? Why or why not?

My Values

01	What are the things you value in life? What are your priorities?

02	List the three most important things for you. Things that give your life meaning.

03	What do you value most about yourself?

04	What needs to shift to make yourself your highest priority?

What do people see?

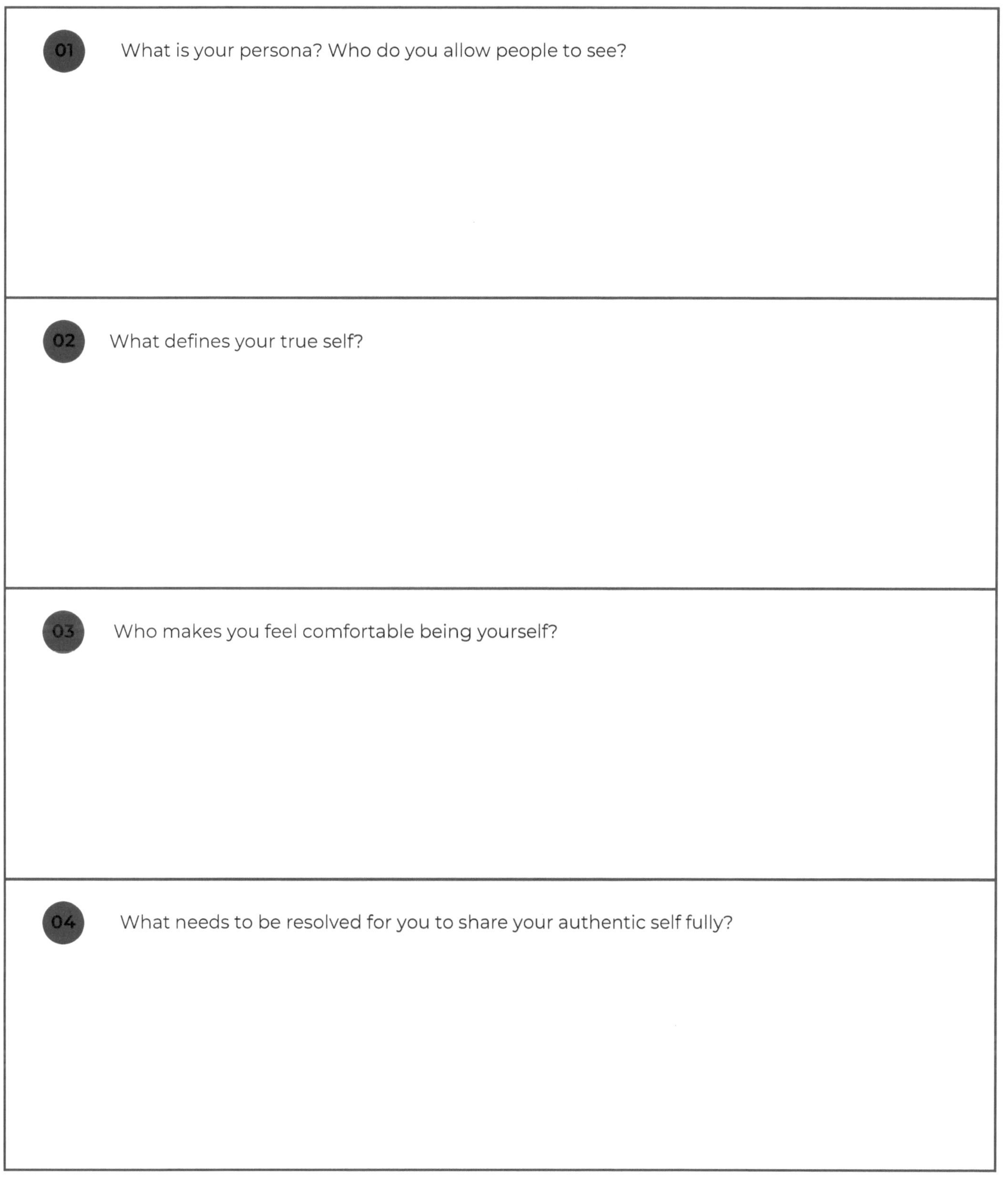

01   What is your persona? Who do you allow people to see?

02   What defines your true self?

03   Who makes you feel comfortable being yourself?

04   What needs to be resolved for you to share your authentic self fully?

Role Models

06 Who are the three people you admire the most?
(Both people you know and don't know personally)

01	02	03

07 Why do you think you admire them?

01	02	03

08 What three traits do you share?

09 What do you appreciate about yourself?

10 How do you share what you appreciate about yourself?

01	02	03

My Patterns

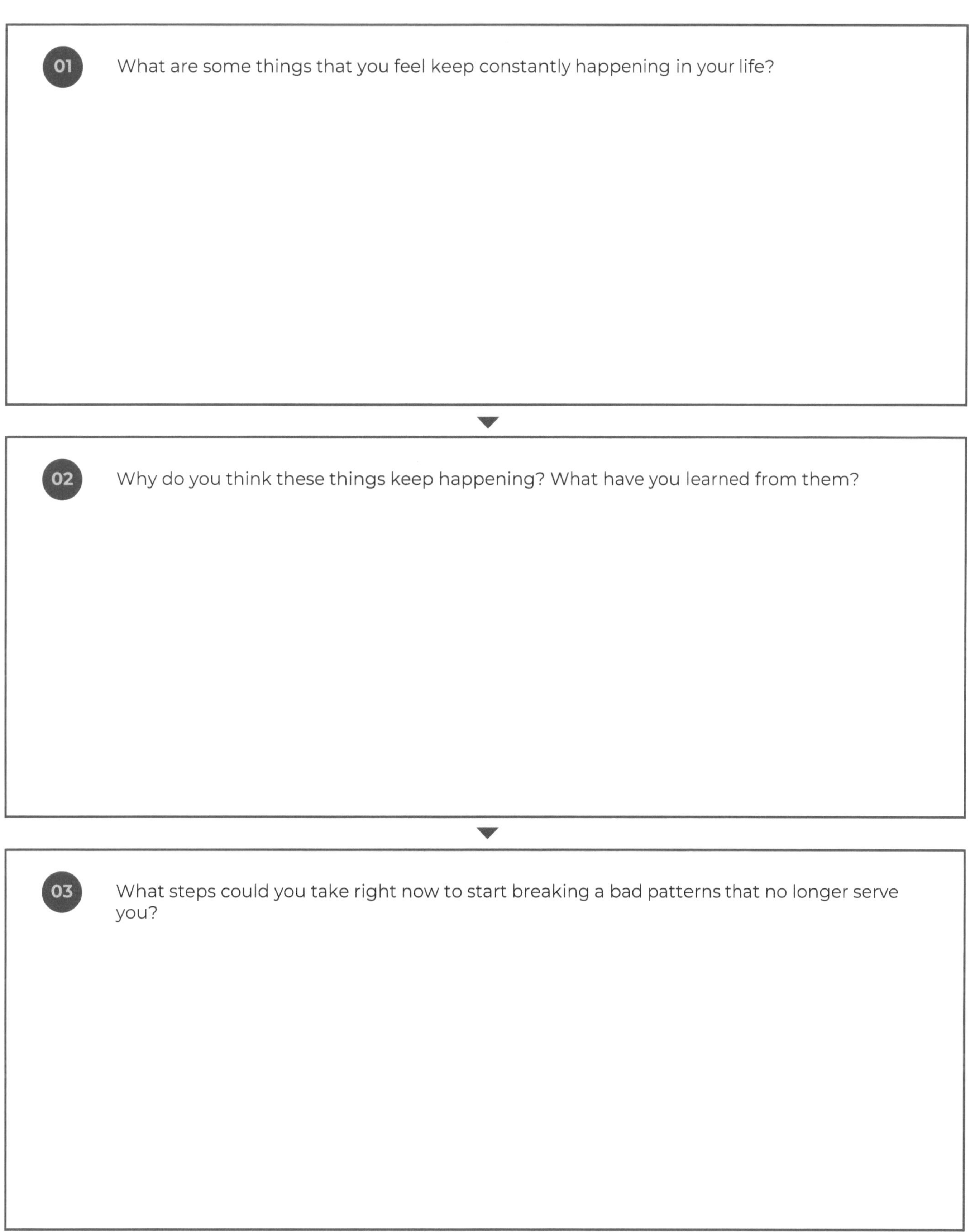

01 What are some things that you feel keep constantly happening in your life?

02 Why do you think these things keep happening? What have you learned from them?

03 What steps could you take right now to start breaking a bad patterns that no longer serve you?

Self Awareness... How do you respond when 'ish happens?

01 What common themes do you see in your reactions? Is it mostly the same? How do others see it? Ask someone if you are not clear about what your reactions look like.

02 How are these reactions holding you back? What steps can you take to overcome them?

03 How do you feel after you react or respond in this way? How do you think you could change it?

How do you feel?

PART ONE

Directions:

Use the feelings wheel below to help you identify the emotional space you often occupy. On the next page, you'll be able to understand more deeply why you're experiencing certain emotions and triggers. Knowing is the first step on the road to healing.

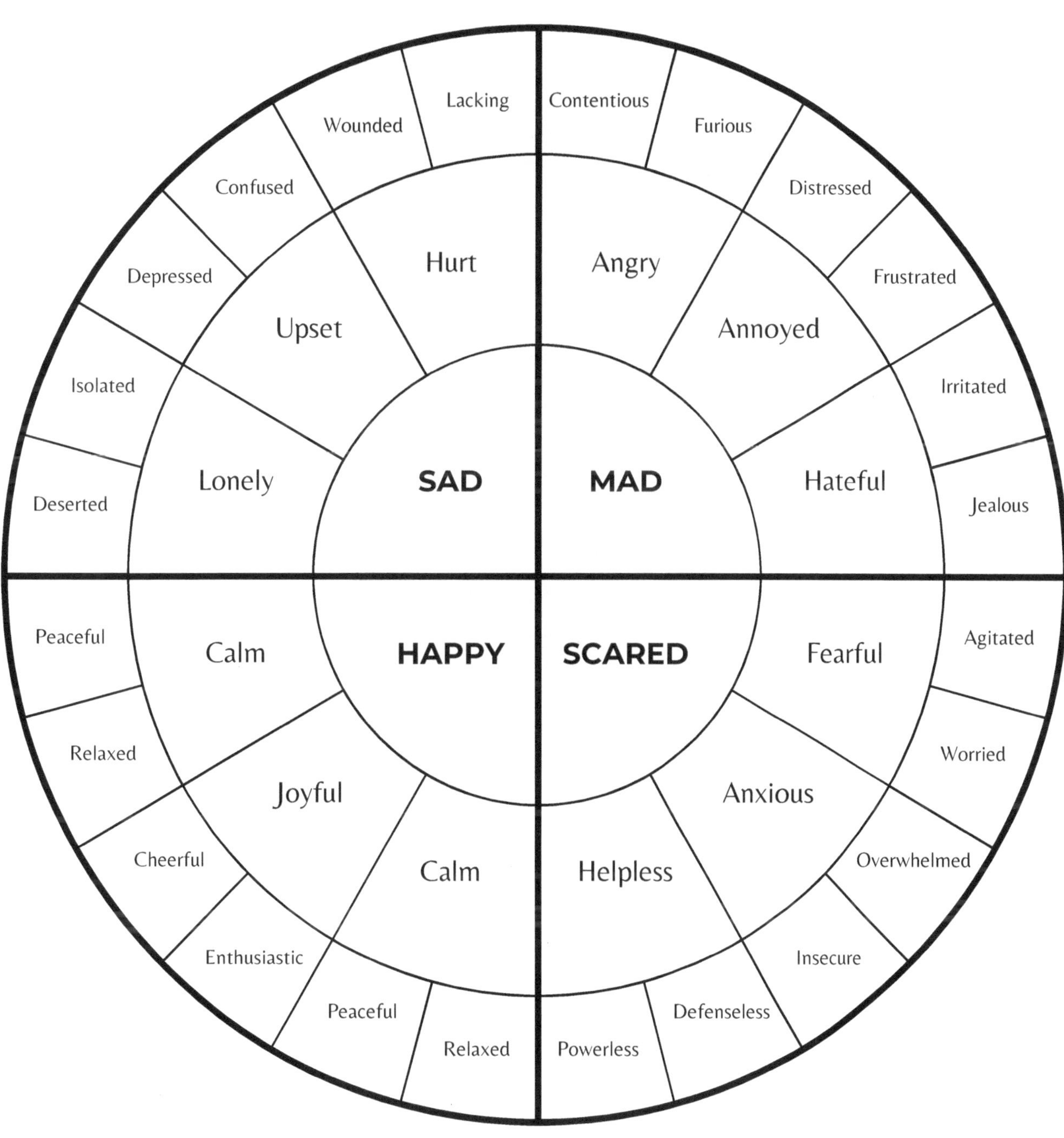

How do you feel?

PART TWO

01 What are the recurring emotion you're constantly feeling?

02 What are the main triggers for this emotion? (Certain people, places, situations etc)
Why do you think these triggers have such an impact?

03 What is the core of your trigger? When was the first time you experienced it?

04   What are the circumstances surrounding the first time you experienced your triggers?

05   What are the main triggers for this emotion? (Certain people, places, situations, etc) Why do you think these triggers have such an impact?

06   Are you ready to forgive the events and people surrounding the triggers? Why or Why not?

Sis, What do you need?

Directions:

To feel free and safe we have certain needs. We must know how to communicate what we need clearly. We have provided a starter list of words to help you share your needs. Of Course, there are more words you can use, but start here. There's no limit on how many you can select! After you've identified the needs, answer the questions below to clarify what each of the needs means to you. Be honest with yourself and take your time. Like grand ma said, ' a closed mouth don't get fed.'

adventure	spiritual fulfillment	feeling love	being loved
accepted by others	stability	order	getting attention
achieving success	status	feeling safe	feeling relaxed
belonging	power	having fun	personal growth
being admired	being respected	being wealthy	being useful
being right	getting noticed	being recognized	being in control
being in control	feeling worthy	fulfilling work	being included
creativity	being valued	expressing yourself	supported by others
empowered	make people happy	feeling alive	being independent
frienship	make people laugh	self development	feeling needed
family	intimacy	free time	being unique

01 Write down your needs and what these mean do you?

02 What steps can you take to fulfill these needs?

Ready to let it go!

01 How long have you been holding on to your pain and what do you need to let go?

02 Who do you need to forgive? What are you forgiving them for?

03 What do you need to forgive yourself for?

04 What is your forgiveness gameplan?

Dreams Bigger
PART ONE

01 What do you want to create in your life?

02 What is your dream lifestyle?

03 What mountains do you have to move for it to happen?

04 Do you believe it is possible? Why or why not?

Dream Bigger
PART TWO

05 How is the life of your dreams different than the life you are living now? What are three habits you need to change to start the dream life process?

06 What commitments do you need to make to yourself to actualize your dreams?

07 What is the cost in one/five/ten years if you do not take these actions to change your life and live your dreams?

The Introduction Exercise

Directions:

Now that you have discovered more about yourself and have more clarity and understanding of who you truly are, you can introduce yourself to others in a whole new way. As if you are it's your lifetime achievement award and millions are listening.. Express all that you want the world to know about you. Your story, what you have overcome , achievements and your legacy. The life you dream to live.

01   What is a moment that makes you most proud?

02   Am I happy with the direction my life is going? What could I improve? What did I achieve?

03   Plan your legacy by considering what you want to be remembered for and take steps to make it happen. It's never too early to start building your legacy.

Notes

Notes

Notes

Notes

Notes

Notes

Notes

Notes

Notes

Notes

Notes

Notes

Notes

Notes

THANK YOU,

Monica Wisdom